The Presents II

Jessica Flynn

Gotham Books

30 N Gould St.
Ste. 20820, Sheridan, WY 82801
https://gothambooksinc.com/

Phone: 1 (307) 464-7800

© 2024 *Jessica Flynn*. All rights reserved.

No part of this book may be reproduced, stored in a retrieval system, or transmitted by any means without the written permission of the author.

Published by Gotham Books (November 19, 2024)

ISBN: 979-8-3305-8403-1 (P)
ISBN: 979-8-3305-8404-8 (E)

Because of the dynamic nature of the Internet, any web addresses or links contained in this book may have changed since publication and may no longer be valid.

The views expressed in this work are solely those of the author and do not necessarily reflect the views of the publisher, and the publisher hereby disclaims any responsibility for them.

Contents

Prologue vii
Evermore 1
The Presents 2
The Best of Times 4
Welcome Sweet Springtime 7
My Tiny-Elusive-White Butterfly 9
My Birthday 10
Whisper in the Wind 11
April is the Sweetest Month 13
A Fleeting Moment 14
A True Friend 16
Jammin' with Jazz 17
'Is There a Cat Heaven' 18
Good Night Dear Felix 19
It's so Sad 21
'Sandy'—October 29, 2012 22
The Longest Night (Hurricane Irene—2012) 23
High School Reunion 25
Life Without my Computer 26
Forty Days 27
True Appraisal of a Man 28
A Pure Heart 29
He Was Her Beau 30
Lonely Shores 31
A Thanksgiving Toast 32

A Week of Sighs	33
What is Christmas?	34
A Champion Mother	35
A Christmas Glaze	38
Faith and Hope	39
Twenty-Five	40
Shining Star	41
2014	43
The Power of Love'	44
A letter from my 'Hero'…. whom I remember Always	45
December 13	47
"Good Night—"	48
"Thoughts Before Battle" (In praise of Heroes)	49
Forever Sunshine	52
ODE TO LISA	54
TEN-TEN TWENTY-ONE	55
April 13, 1965 - December 19, 2022	59
Sequestration	61
"If You Forget Me"	64
Enjoying Life 'Whatever Age you're told to act' Darrel Sifford (Phila.Inq.) 1955	65
'The Story of Life'	67
My Calendar	68
About the Author	70

Dedicated with love to my many inspirations on the journey of life.

**Live the life you love—love the life you live
And
Embrace 'The Presents'**

Prologue

THE PRESENTS

Poetry, words and images—are a transcendence of life, events and special people in

'The Presents'.

It is also a dedication to all the Tommy's Johnny's and Jane's who were unable to fulfill their lives and dreams because of their 'supreme sacrifice'. Our memories of them are a 'Present' and an homage to their immortality. I am humbly honored to write an 'addition' to my life's book as a tribute to 'Tommy's' written request of his dreams—— though life's transience was inconceivable at the time.

'One day you will take my heart completely and make it more fiery than a dragon.

Your eyelashes will write on my heart the poem that could never come from the pen of any poet." — Jalal Uddin Rumi (12071273)

Evermore

The Presents

Cherish the presents Of love, joy and lessons learned from pain

Treasured moments in a lifetime

Sieve through our hands As grains of sand.

So easy to take for granted

The gifts life has handed

Searching unknowingly Far and wide – over land and seas. Cannot be found

In the silk of India

White marble of Italy

In caviar, 'escargot' (go)

Or refined gemstones from

The ground.

The presents are the gifts

Sent from God above

The days, sunshine & moments

Shared with those you love, Their looks, their words & laughter,

Memories ever after

Which time cannot erase

Shared in the heartfelt present

As in the windswept blossoms

Which slowly wing away
Will kiss your cheek –
And—without a trace
Rest a smile upon your face.

The Best of Times

The best of times,
Somehow—are now.
In many ways—
Who would have thought
Or even sought—
To know that,
The world we live in
Would become smaller.
We're talking to friends,
And even brand-new relatives
From computer-screen to places
We'd never dream of going,
Looking into their psyches,
Knowing their 'likes'—'unlikes'
Sometimes see their faces smile
All the while, we get to know
Who they are, some insignificant
And some challenging momentous
Feats they have accomplished,
Send wishes and prayers
That we may share, Empathize, sympathize—and
yes – We really care!

It's inexpensive & even cooler
As the world keeps getting smaller
To have friends who live in Norway
Sweden, Thailand, and Italy,
They send their love and kisses,
When away for a day— They even miss us!
We enjoy sharing music videos
Talk of favorite TV shows,
Current news, political views Yesterday's and today's.
Each morning, look forward to the
Status they may send
Enjoy comments & information
Picturesque images that they post
From near and far—perhaps –
Of unexpected
Asteroids or shooting stars from coast to coast!
It's so much fun for everyone
Sharing holiday—birthday greetings
Congratulations—engagements. Talk of TV shows, favorite teams
Some aspirations and dreams.
We are all significant
Whatever we may write inspiring—or—trite.
A reality of the times and The common civilization of

People here and diverse nations.
Reaching out & friendship craved,
The broad imminence of humanity Which has presently been paved.
A mutual bond of friendship gleans
Yes,—I believe
Here, there, and everywhere—
The best of times are now
Behind my eighteen-inch computer screen—
Somehow !—

Welcome Sweet Springtime

The frost is off the pumpkin
Hints of grassy green
Beneath the winter snow
Eagerly awaiting Peeking shyly thru the dank wet earth To craft its grand debut Of hope which springs eternal
And maintain its promise true.
The song of robins through the trees The humming of butterflies and bees
Harmonizing a symphony of joy
Enthralled by budding floral toys.
Classes dismissed for springtime break
Some moments in time to recreate
Backyard parties—wedding 'I do's' Fun with friends and barbecues.
And all the while gives rise to smiles
Welcome Sweet Springtime—-
Come on in– Please stay awhile! –

Please do not intrude!

My Tiny-Elusive-White Butterfly

My tiny elusive white butterfly
Always flying 'round me
Sometimes low—at times high,
Tapping flippantly on my shoulder,
Encircling around in my space Imparting a smile to my face.
Is it your way of saying hello—
Or—'I would like to know you,
And share this bright summer day,
Though you flap your wings and sashay away?
For a moment or two you settle
Upon a flower with vibrant petal,
But only too soon go dancing away
To the rhythm of your own drummer,
Sharing your exquisiteness
With the sun-drenched days of summer!

My Birthday

It is a beautiful day today Hooray!

The sun is shining—feeling great, Thanking God with a sigh—for Presents one cannot buy.

Health, joy, family and friends Unconditional love that has no end.

It's a special day today,

The ninth of April –

A holiday today – 'Easter Monday',

'Phillies' come home to play,

And best of all—

It's

My Birthday!! Hooray!!!

(written 4/9/2013)

Whisper in the Wind

Like a whisper in the wind.

In springtime love did bloom, Its fragrance so very sweet— But vanished—all too soon.

She sought to find it once again With troubled mind and heavy heart. This springtime love had been a dream Reality was dark—it seemed.

Like a whisper in the wind,

Again she heard its call, She followed reluctantly The music down the hall.

It was springtime once again,

Its fragrance just as sweet— They kept dancing all night long To the rhythm and its beat.

Like that whisper in the wind

And the sound so resonating Love's renaissance of wedded bliss A time for celebrating!

April is the Sweetest Month

Chocolate eggs & Easter bunnies,

Homemade cookies topped w/honeys, A young man's fancy turns to love And April Showers from above.

Flowers are bursting from their beds,

As resurrected—no longer dead,

The trees are dressed in shades of green— A presentation just fit for queens!

Clocks turned back—the days are long,

Birthday parties and lots of song, Strawberry, chocolate & cheesecake—too, Personalized for me and you.

A festive time for celebration, Thanking God –in appreciation.

Yes—

April is the sweetest month!

A Fleeting Moment

I heard two voices in the night

Though their faces out of sight, A fleeting moment of destined fate They weren't tired—tho' it was late. He drove his car on numerous rides, From New York to New Jersey side. Their lives a whirlwind of fun and dates They weren't tired—though it was late.

Came time to take a final stand, Ask the padre for her hand. He couldn't miss this closing chance Of love—forever—and romance.

His dream of happiness came true, Married to Kim with eyes of blue. Then—fast forward to their precious boys—

Their presence—a constant joy

A fleeting moment of destined fate – They weren't tired—though it was late.

A True Friend

I have a friend who's always there
To lend a helping hand
When I'm troubled and things go wrong,
She seems to understand

We share our many thoughts and feelings— We sometimes even giggle—and laugh at little things,

As though we were still teenagers—we even dance and sing

I've known her since she was a child, We've blazed through land and water.

Her beauty unreviled and cannot be denied.

I feel so lucky and declare everyone 'ought-er Have a true friend—as my lovely thoughtful daughter.

Jammin' with Jazz

I know an 'artiste' from San Jose'
And many instruments she does play—
Harp, cello, and the saxophone
Pop, jazz, or classical—in varied tones
Occasionally her 'CD' comes my way
Pulsating jazz that swings and sways
Pizzicato, andante or allegro beat,
Captivating music to my dancing feet!
Reminiscent of my high school days
When the second violin I endeavored
No comparison for sure—nevertheless I'm motivated
and re-verberated to sing a happy song
and perhaps—
just dance along!

'Is There a Cat Heaven'

Pitter Patter—and a special knocking at your door, He loved this life and wanted more. Is there a cat heaven—I hope so Or—is paradise bogus—I want to know!

His request was only to survive,

To bring me joy and stay alive,

To walk, jump, run, eat and drink of water, Small request—in any order!

Though he fell, crashed, fought to stay, All too soon was taken away. A special knocking at your door— 'It's Felix—my cat –do not ignore!

To turn away would be your sin – Open the door and let him in!' Is there a cat heaven—I sure hope so— Or is it bogus—- I need to know!

Good Night Dear Felix

The house is full of you –

Everywhere I turn

A lesson to be learned

Of life and death,

From your omnipotent presence Until your last breath.

I look down upon the tower of my computer Where you'd recline for many hours.

I visualize your eyes of glistening green Their hypnotic beauty, their mystic stare, Seem to follow me everywhere!

With trepidation, down the basement steps I tread,
No frolicsome friend racing to be fed. The bowl of water still waiting there

At its service—your absence unaware.

You were serene with an occasional purr,

Content with life and your routine,

Enjoying the whistle and songs I'd sing, Hermetically to my soul you'd cling.

Suddenly, your smooth tri-colored form Withered, and weakened—then wasted away.

In vain—I fought to weather that storm With love, milk—silk scarves to keep you warm. But you drifted away and out of sight – With tear-filled eyes—'Good-Night dear Felix'!

It's so Sad

It's so sad—that people are bad,
Children abandoned in their homes
All alone—wondering why So much love they've been denied.
Raggedy clothes, dirty hair,
Mocked and sneered at—by their peers, So intimidating—but they try
To ignore those hurts—and taunts defy.
They hang around in the streets Looking for love— and something to eat.
Because their search is unfulfilled, They steal, they lie—take pills for thrills . . . And sometimes kill!
Innocent lives destroyed
In their world of little joy
It's too late to change ill fate—but
It's so sad—- that people are bad
If only someone had offered their hand And taken time to understand!

'Sandy'—October 29, 2012

Made it through the night,
Power still on with a sense of
Calm outside,
No wind gusts or pelting rain—yet!
'She's' gone away—though we shall not forget Her wrath—the path—of mass destruction left behind,
As we pick up fallen pieces,—exhale—and unwind.
'Go away—Stay away Sandy!
It's Halloween—no more mischief please!
Time for apples, chocolates
And—'lots of candy!'

The Longest Night (Hurricane Irene—2012)

After the longest night of rain, wind & fright,
The lights are still on
The sump-pump still pumping
It's Sunday Morning At six-twenty-five We're alive!
Thank God!!!!
The car is in the driveway,
Shiny and silver, free of debris Fallen trees or branches— Thank God!!!
The house—its rooms still standing,
Roof and bricks intact,
Defying 'Irene's' turbulence And not a single crack.— Thank God!!!
I call family & friends via telephone.
So grateful of their salvation as my very own.
Tho' millions suffered with unrelenting pain,
With our benevolence and help—their restoration gained.! Thank God!!!
The present is such a gift;—sometimes we're unaware
Until a disaster strikes—then—really scared,
Too soon reminded within our hearts,

How we are truly blessed and must savor Those simple little joys in our individual quests And appreciate profoundly their magnificence!

Thank God!

High School Reunion

So glad to be here,

Let's give a cheer,

"Our journey of a thousand miles"

Has led us home—unreviled,

With stories of joy, fortune and love Entwined with twinges of life's strain And sometimes—pain.

But on this road of many miles,

We've gained 'wisdom with age'—they say,

Some pounds, 'laugh-lines' along the way,

But most of all—we're the lucky ones, We've come back to South Philly We can laugh, reminisce and be silly!

We've arrived—We're alive!

With warm memories of yesteryear

Journey's 'first step' date –

Seems so long ago—we know Let's raise our glasses and give a cheer, For friends both here—and over there.

Let's thank God—for all he gives "Love life—drink of life's fullness, and take all it can give.

Love life and every moment must count – Glory in its honor

And revel in its font!"

Life Without my Computer

Ohh—how I miss my computer!
Gone away for repair,
For me—it was my scooter
Taking me 'here' and 'there'.
Two days without—is much too long,
Minus e-mails, 'Facebook' and 'Utube' songs,
Unable to produce my photo shows
From my favorite pictures,
Devoid of vital statistics,
My poetry and prose
That only 'Mr. Computer' knows.
Finally—he is back!
Hope he stays awhile
Without a scratch or sneeze.
Welcome Home—no more 'Viruses—please!

Forty Days

One never knows when love walks in. To turn away would be a sin, In forty days my life has changed. My place on earth all rearranged, The sun & stars are all in place. Yet more radiant—with diamonds And jewels in my space.

With obstacles at first meeting,

And time too quickly fleeting,

He was lost but persevered

Never faltered, never feared Until the moment of 'Hello'

Was it that moment at first sight,

Seems redundant and maybe trite,

Springtime—or the month of May

'Cinco de Mayo' or 'Margarita' Or light flirtation with 'Senorita'?

No one knows or can state

Fascination or destined fate A prized and prophetic day

And we refuse to turn away!!

True Appraisal of a Man

True appraisal of a man
Is not the heart-shaped diamond ring
Or the love songs that he sings, But the beating heart inside When love is sorely tried.
A flagrant moment unexpected,
When one would least suspect it,
Furtively comes your way, When; where and how— One cannot say.
Does your 'Sir Galahad' evoke
His prized velvet cloak— Or insensitive to your pain
Quickly turn away and wane,
Seeking selfish gratification Indifferent to your trepidation.
The heart-shaped diamond ring
Will lose its shimmery glow—
Instantly you will know
That the beating heart inside
Is merely tin and mummified, And with eyes open wide
Love's prolongation—denied!

A Pure Heart

My love is not for sale,

Tho' many have tried to buy it—or steal, With diamonds & gifts as a ruse, To deceive and plot their subterfuge.

A pure heart is what I'm looking for, I'm apathetic to golden lure.

If you cannot walk the dicey roads Of startling thorns that love implodes.

Many a lass has been mistook By unveiled guise of a stealthy crook..

I cautiously on this road retread

With pearls of wisdom—avow— 'a glass of wine

A loaf of bread!'—

Sans thou—

'True paradise enow' !

He Was Her Beau

Remembering—long ago,

She was his girl,

He was her beau. They vowed to love each other In sickness and in health. Love was their joy, Joy was their wealth.

She was his wife In happiness and strife. He was her buddy, She was his life.

Always looked glad, Never seemed sad.

Living their Camelot

And sharing their thrill Of being together On Lafayette Hill.

Exactly sixty years ago—on October 11,

The date they were wed— He was called from Camelot To Paradise—instead!

Let's toast & raise a glass of wine

To their unwavering love

Today—and from its budding start,

Though—called away from Camelot He'll live forever—in our hearts.

Lonely Shores

Because I have faith—I will endure,
I will look beyond the darkness—and the clouds
And with the help from above
Will follow the path and promise of tomorrow.
Forever inspired by God's wonder and His glory,
Rejoicing the new dawn and starry nights— I'm sure I will endure – Because I have faith!

A Thanksgiving Toast

Thank You God for thy bounty
The green grass, earth, & air
The sun, moon, stars from above
Remind me daily of your love
Whether here or 'over there'
I know your guiding light is near.
Sharing the 'taters', turkey & pie,
Together with family & friends
A wonderful time to be living We raise our glasses high.
In unison—together we shout— God Bless us everyone and
Happy Thanksgiving!

A Week of Sighs

A week of sighs –

Trying to go on with Christmas cheer, Couldn't feel it anywhere. Our hearts were heavy

And thoughts worrisome,

A family friend had fallen ill Every day—more terrible.

Doctors were perplexed,

One diagnosis and then—- the next,

Could it be 'pneumonia

Or pleurisy or gall bladder, Blood, liver, or even kidney stones, Varied messages 'via phone'.

We hoped and prayed for a solution,

Curable treatment and diminution Of infection undetected, The worst of them suspected.

A week has past,

He's home at last,

Mysterious illness has been found!

Health—with treatment—will resound.

Family and friends by our side,

Prayers answered from above, To celebrate this gift of love.

With thankful hearts we give a cheer—

Merry Christmas to All—and Happy New Year//////

What is Christmas?

Christmas is children

Christmas is snow

Music and laughter Wherever we go.

Singing of carols In churches and streets

Eating Cookies with honey. Candy canes & sweets.

Remembering our friends

With presents and greetings

Planning for travel, parties & meetings Shopping & wearing our bright colored dresses Upswept hairdo's and decorative tresses.

Sharing a toast by a fireplace

Reflecting a glow in a loved one's face

Embracing our memories of yesteryear With heartfelt warmth, a smile— and sometimes a tear.

My present for family, friends,

Each girl and each boy

A wish for health, happiness & joy

But—most of all—

Christmas is light from heaven above

Announcing His birth—and Eternal Love.

A Champion Mother

It was on this day –
The twelfth of December –
Tho' too many years ago,
My memory piques of
A champion lady—my Mother
Passed from this world to another.
I always remember
She was strong, loving and kind Many thoughts run through my mind,
Deeply devoted to my Father, Sister. Brother and I. The love she exuded No money can buy.
When we were sick with a cold or the 'flu'.
She knew exactly what to do
Homemade chicken soup,

And freshly 'squozen' orange juice.
Stay in bed with warm covers,
Magical antiseptic
To ease muscular aches and pains, And our energy regain.
Three or more times a day =
She'd climb upstairs with meds & food,
Would take our temperatures –
Tell a story, make us smile
Rest & recuperation—'Mommy's' style !!
Just one of the many wonderful recollections
Of my Mom—her warmth, her laughter,
Treasured 'ever after
By me and my lucky family!
Thank you Mom—We Love You !!!
Always near—but wish you were here!

A Christmas Glaze

I'm painting a glaze

Over the haze of pain and strife Happening in life.

There is little joy for the unemployed And Santa's are sad cause they have no toys For some little girls and boys.

But it's the Christmas season, The bells are ringing, Choirs of children singing.

A season to be jolly—mistletoe and holly, And nothing should go wrong.

Tho' headlines scream of ugly crimes

Rape, burglaries and homicides, Impoverished people seeking food, The homeless searching for a hood.

Husbands fighting with their wives

Ignoring the anguish of children's cries,

Their vows of love—so long ago Have melted like the drifting snow.

Soldiers marching off to war Will not return as were before. Those who wait are filled with pain Hoping to see them once again.

But the luminous glow on Christmas Eve

Gives all reason to believe The glaze we feel this silent night— Rekindles the spirit and hope burns bright.

Faith and Hope

Heard a robin's song, saw a blue jay
Sending warm thoughts to you today
In the midst of life's trials and travails
Hope you find your 'Holy Grail'
At times you may be inundated
At the thorny obstacles created
Along the pathway of your dreams— Yet—find positive reinforcement—
From the flowing steady streams.
Spring is happening over all,
Melted snow, green grass tall
Languishing willows, fragrant billows
Release anxieties & stress
As your spirits soar—calling you 'Al fresco' to attend and complement the awakening of nature's roar.

Twenty-Five

All that I am…. this much I know
The joy I've felt in watching you grow
From babe in arms, to cheerful child Beguiled by your charming smile.
Too soon you reached bewitching teens
In a little while—'twenty-five'
Wit and charm, chic and styled
You've set many hearts afire
Hold fast to truth and self-esteem
Follow the pathway of your dreams
Delighted to hold you in my heart With pride, joy and love though miles apart.

Shining Star

When he was eight
We had a date
We'd stop at Dunkin' Donuts And buy some cake
He liked Video Games
That was his thing
'Game Stop'—next door Made his heart sing.
Simple pleasures and joys
For the heart of a boy And the look on his face
Completely irreplaceable!
Time always takes its bow
Events are much different now Separated by many miles
He studies, works—a different style!

He visits with me once in while
Handsome—tall—, a charming smile,
Sometimes calls on telephone
Near or far—my shining star Makes my heart smile!
☺

2014

Ring out the old,

Bring in the new Dismiss the false.

Hold fast the true. A time made for singing, A new year is winging.

A pure spotless slate

To recreate

Some resolutions,

Some diets,

Lots of dreams

Don't hesitate,

A new year awaits—

Believe—go forward With faith, hope and love and a glass of champagne. Or chug down a beer, or maybe two

Ring out the old,

Bring in the new—

Celebrate !

2014 is waiting for you!

The Power of Love'

Love has the power to dispel death—and while you can't make the fact of death go

away you can try to dispel the power that death can cast over our present and our future.

When you do that for someone else through a thoughtful act or a moment when you show

love and compassion—you have given THAT PERSON an extra gift –

And through love they live'

'anonymous'

A letter from my 'Hero'…. whom I remember Always

from: Tommy

He honored me with his words dreams and hopes of tomorrows that ended abruptly. Today I honor his memory. his written words, and love.

"Dearest:

I'm hoping that you receive this letter on Valentine's day.

Do you know that it's hard to compare you to anything but I think I finally have found you to be like a good book and I fall more and more in love with you as I turn each page and as I finish each chapter I know that the next will be better than the last. It's a LONG BOOK and I hope it lasts forever—and like a good book—you leave an impression on all who read and love you—and for every minute I spend in the joy of thinking of you I get to love, understand and appreciate you a little more and— perhaps some day I'll be able to give the love and happiness you deserve and be able to pay for the honor to be able to say you are mine; and some day be able to thank you for a pocket size addition to the book case . . .

With all my love and devotion –

I am yours now and forever—for indeed I sure want to be. /s/

Tommy

(His life and 'his book' cut short—but his memory is cherished! He left 'an impression on me and this is my tribute to the power of love. It is a 'long book' after all—and lasts forever!

December 13

"Dearest

Do you know how much I miss not being with you this Xmas and New Years. I'll tell you, I miss you so much that although it's still a long ways off—I know that Xmas night I'll lie in bed and try to fall asleep—I'll have a rather sad feeling inside me and I'll have a lonely little tear in my eye. It will be lonely for you, for your smiling face and all the rest of the nice things that make you 'Jessie'. I hope you think about me at the same time and remember that I love you very deeply . . .

Honey, you said you loved me now more than ever and that some day you'd tell me why. If you don't tell me in your next letter—I'm going to ask you when I get home. I imagine you had a personal experience that was the cause of what you said. Good Night for now.

/s/Love, Tom . . . .
Merry Xmas

(The following week—December 20—he was killed when he accidentally stepped on a landmine.) However—somehow, somewhere,—he must know!

"Good Night—"

How I hate those words—the nights!—days! hrs. mins. were wasted alone –

After we said those words to each other! If I could only have a few of them back –

But if given a few. I'd want more and more (all eternity, all!

So

All my Love

/s/ Tommy

(without the Good Night for there is nothing good without you and all time is night until you bring day again)"

"Thoughts Before Battle"
(In praise of Heroes)

While I lie darkly in the pit of night

Alert for what grim fate might be in store,

I seem to hear an avalanche of sound And then, I hear no more

Till softly, like a vast advancing host

To find me in the darkness where I lie, A million peepers as in boyhood days Arrive to sing their old sweet lullaby.

Upon my shoulders where the straps cut deep

To etch their patterns of dull pain,

I feel the gentle touch of something warm, And very kind, like rain;

Then joyfully she laughs with lips of rose, To kiss my wild and unbelieving eyes

To whisper life and home and kids And fill with song the menaced skies.

One hour to go before the great barrage

Will cut the heavens with a sword of flame Yet strange that I should dream askance

Of nothing but my own forgotten name,

To see it as I carved it long ago

On that great oak upon the hill

And feel the bark's strong fingers hold me
Hug me, want me, love me still !"
(anonymous)

Frozen in Time

On a cold January day
Into backyard I did stray. I walked into gazebo
To sweep the fallen snow,
Was touched & elated
When quickly I did see
Two snowy- white heart-prints
Impressed into the floor
Glistening & starkly glaring toward me
The other snow—with sunshine
Had melted away
But the heart-prints stayed,
As though this was a message
Sent from someone up above
A pre-valentine greeting,
Bringing to mind
A love of long-ago
Expressing, remembering
And…. frozen in sunshine!

Forever Sunshine

You were my all The world to me To the world—A hero.

A name on the wall

To Me—

A luminescent light

Burning bright Heart and spirit to mine And Forever Sunshine.

ODE TO LISA

She is fair of face and wise in ways
With a spirit undaunted by praise,
He acts gallantly both day and night
Let your heart to him take flight.

There will be others with might and force,
Who promise riches but yield remorse,
And hopefully, you'll wave them on
For only, too soon, their glitter is on.

But – if he offers a heart that is true,
May this virtue capture you.

TEN-TEN TWENTY-ONE

And what a, magical day It was!
My day 'in the 'sun'!!!

Meticulously & surreptitiously crafted
To the 'umpteenth' & intricate degree
By Lisa & my – 'Accomplice –Family'.
As I was Chauffeured by smiling Jim -
driven to the ritzy 'River Winds'
And before my star-struck eyes
My very own magical episode

Winding UP THE YELLOW BRICK ROAD

A SEA OF FRIENDLY FACES OF YESTERDAYS & TODAYS!

Pleasantly surprised to see 'Singer 'D'Atoli' from 'The Mansion' of long ago who seemed to reappear as in a dream! His countenance, melodious voice &, my wonderment   a reason to cheer.

Etched within my heart –

EACH AND EVERY ONE OF YOU

'donned in finery with presents &

your radiance captivating

, and in unison - All celebrating "

Me' 'YOU', &

LIFETIME Memories &

The Day That I Was Born.

And it must be stated; delayed & therefore belated celebration

Post-vaccination & CoVid19 Hibernation

So, gratified at a jubilation of music, dancing & drum rolls!

Elated to hear dear friend Tony and (former 'Elvis Impersonator) dedicate his rendition of 'The Wonder of You; -- to me!!! (thank U □)

Photo Booths – Hats & 'Limoncello Favors (crafted
by 'Jessica B. Schultz) recalling a favorite message
'When life gives you lemons – Make 'limoncello'!
Tables all decorated w/ brightly colored s yellowcress

Top of the line food --, Tasty appetizers-

A fountain of champagne & wine

'SIMPLY DIVINE'!

I felt somewhat surreal & mellow

w/ a toast to all for 'Cent 'Anni' w/ me

symbolic; 'Limoncello'!!

Thanking God

For the blessings of a lifetime

My daughter Lisa who secretly & diligently crafted

This 'superb & magical day1!

Anthony & Kathy

& their precious gifts of Anthony David, Erica w/
'Princess Julie Anna

Jessica & Matt were there in loving spirit w/ 'Stella'
our new born regal shining star

There was Dora along w/ Ana & Jo

It must be stated: – We're All vaccinated! It's been a
long long year

w/ poignant memories of Elmer –Mom & Poppy in heaven above Whose guidance & nurturing harbor gratitude & love!

SO MANY CHERISHED FRIENDS – I REVEL IN ITS FOUNT

AND THANK GOD ABOVE

For this day & blessed celebration

Of Life, Love & Memories

That evoke the moment when

Lisa led me hand in hand

to this momentous episode

'A sea of friendly faces'

Upon my very own

Magical & 'Magnificent

YELLOW BRICK ROAD'

April 13, 1965 - December 19, 2022

Lisa, my daughter – my best friend
Address: 'Heaven's Door'

Oh – How I Miss

Those ten A.M. phone calls, conversations, reservations, smiles outings, nudges,

Stops at Friendly's for favorite sundaes topped w/ whipped cream &

'Vanilla Fudgs'.

Reminiscing & remembering those summer vacations, Cruises to Europe for historical 'rest & recreation'.

Your camaraderie luncheons w/ friends & always on the run

Upon your return

Always stated' It was fun!'

Always dressed to the nines
manicured   nails long & flowing per hair-dos &looking so fine

You cared, you shared the joy of life w/friends & family

Suddenly & surreptitiously taken from Us & 'Me'

To lighten & brighten the heavens above w/ your joyful spirit & eternal love

Radiating from afar!

Yes Lisa – I agree

It is

Absolutely & Totally Bizarre!

Sequestration

'O Captain My Captain
Your heartfelt job is done
Your nerves have weathered every storm
"The prize you sought was won!"

Friends all gathered here
Raise their glasses high
To Jeff, Amos, Ken , -- Lisa
and the other 'guys'
Who gave their strength & sinew
In the present and the past.

This fervent toast we send
Be happy Be proud– it's you we crown
Forward - Onward –Have a blast!!
Though Incredible -- and surely unforgettable
"You're Free At Last!"

"If You Forget Me"

'If each day a flower climbs up to your lips to see me,
In me all that fire is repeated
In me—nothing is extinguished or forgotten.

Pablo Neruda

Enjoying Life 'Whatever Age you're told to act' Darrel Sifford (Phila.Inq.) 1955

The boy looked to be about 4 or 5. He was in the grocery store and was acting like the legendary bull in a china shop. He was into everything; talking to all around him; giggling and acting silly At first the mother just ignored his antics—but later she couldn't take it anymore—so she screamed in a full measure of fury : The boy was told to "Act your age". The boy flinched as if he'd been burnt. I watched them go with a feeling of sadness that I didn't immediately understand. As I played it back in my mind—I understood why I felt that sadness—cause he WAS acting his age with his usual childish curiosity and high energy! His mother was telling him to grow up—to behave as SHE wanted him to; as a sober adult—and not a free spirited little boy! That I believe is the simple reason for sadness!

This doesn't only happen to little boys—for it happens to most of us all of our lives. At this or that age—this or that kind of bathing suit is appropriate—this or that kind of business suit—this or that kind of plaid pants are out because they make you look like a child.

You might want to go back to school and take a course—but what would people think? At your age—you wouldn't have anything in common with anyone—so they would think you were silly. So—you forget about school and just decide to stay home and watch tv.

You might want to buy a bright red car but the salesman looks at you—and says are you sure that you want red—at your age?? No— you need a sedan probably black or dark grey—'dignified'! Life the one over there. We'll be glad to show you a more age appropriate car—just for you!

When you reach a certain age—you can't act like a child anymore — without paying a price—which is that people might think you're irresponsible. You can't be goofy You must be grim—'cause grimness is a mark of 'maturity' of "success'! The more grim you are —the stronger is the signal that you're announcing to the world that 'you've made it'!! How sad it is that so many of us—buy into it—and act as we think is age appropriate…. for people our age.

A while back I came into possession of a self inventory exercise put out by Swain Associates—a list of sentences to be completed by those who want to find out more about who they are; their values, what they stand for.

Some of the questions:

I appreciate about myself… I thought about that one a long time before I answered: "the willingness to march to my own drumbeat, to be my own person; to be unconventional if I feel like it; to be more concerned about what I think of me than what others think of me;

One example of my ability to feel joy the unbridled childlike elation that comes when the catamaran is flying across the bay, when the wind is whistling through the sails; when the sun is hot on my back and the salty air is melting in my mouth,:

One of the happiest periods of my life, when I realized finally that I belonged; that I had paid my dues, that I didn't have to apologize; didn't have to play a role that is was ok to cry if I felt like it—although others might be laughing:

I need to spend more time with "people who enjoy life, who know how to have fun, who like themselves—even when others may be critical of them,"

I need to spend less time with people who are phony because they aren't true to themselves—who don't know who they are because they are in LOCKSTEP with everyone else"

Before I leave this planet I want to 'regress' or 'progress' to childhood again to feel the same freedom and lack of constraints that I felt as a child, the same sense of being carefree, the same confidence that things will work out in ways that are reasonable".

Does the time ever come when we really need to act our age? I don't think so, and I hope not. What do you think????

'The Story of Life'

"Sometimes people come into your life and you know right away that they were meant to be there to serve some sort of purpose, teach you a lesson, or to help you figure out who you are or who you want to become. You never know who these people may be 'but when you lock eyes with them you know at that very moment they will affect your life in some profound way.' But—sometimes the reality and awareness of this person's value is not realized until many years later—- and only then do you see clearly and you fully understand that person's significance and lesson of life.

And sometimes things happen to you that may seem horrible, painful and unfair at first, but in reflection, you find that without overcoming those obstacles you would have never realized your full potential, strength, willpower, or heart.

More importantly—if you love someone tell him or her—for you never know what tomorrow may bring."

"Faith, Hope and Love—and the greatest of these is Love";

The greatest lessons and cherished presents of life!

-anonymous

My Calendar

These special greetings to you I send, Unique & tasty vintage blend:
January brings the snow – Makes our toes and fingers glow.
February—more of same thing, But valentines & candy make our hearts sing.
In March we hear the winds' fury brew. Cause winter has nothing left to do.
Here comes April with promised green Of sprouting grass & leaves on trees Welcome first robin on the scene!
May is waiting all in bloom. Doors of spring are open wide— A fragrant colorful world outside.
In comes June with its lures Of summer vacations &sandy shores. Whether we look or whether we listen Rippling waters murmur and glisten.
In July—Long & delicious days of radiant sun,
Outdoor barbecues & lots of fun.
The dry and parching August heat Breeds red tomatoes & golden wheat.
September's days too soon are here with summer's rest but autumn's cheer,
Colored foliage, apples & wine
A symphony of life entwined.
October's hayrides & Halloween Witches & tiny goblins seen.
November is time for Thanksgiving
Sharing blessings of lives worth living
In December—we appreciate
Friends, family and radiance from above A festive time to celebrate The birth of Jesus and His love.
Let's thank God that we are here,
Merry Christmas to All Happy New Year!
. . . .
With adoration and gratification for 'The Presents'

'And still after all these years the sun has never said to the earth 'you owe me'—— Look what happens with love like that'!

-Rumi

About the Author

Jessica Flynn has written poetry, ever since she was a child of eleven. Her first poem was 'Nature's Serenade' which was an appreciation of a beautiful day in June. She enjoys writing and her feelings are depicted in those moments of motivation and inspiration.

She shares and reads some of her poetry@ historic events, residences and social gatherings. She also received Editor's Choice Awards, nominated previously for Poetry Ambassador of the Year, and has been listed in the International Who's Who in Poetry. Her previous book 'It is Love' was dedicated to her mother and father, — loving and strong influences in her life.

Because of some early tragedies and losses in her twenty's, she has gained an indomitable strength and passion for the appreciation of life and love which she values. However, she longs for the day that all people will live in peace and harmony; love one another, in spite of their differences. That is her dream!

She is retired from various positions. in the U.S. Government service, Signal Corps, U.S. Naval Hospital, National Park Service, Public Health Service and Environmental Protection Agency. She has also worked as a Medical Transcriptionist @ Jefferson Hospital in Philadelphia, PA.

Today – her greatest passions are the blessings of God, —family— traveling, writing, and most of all – The Presents!

'Wan given honorable mention in Free Poetry Contest for poem "He Makes my Heart Smile' which was previously published in 'It is Love' by Jessica Flynn.

Received an 'Outstanding Achievement in Poetry' by the

International Society of Great Poets in 2007.'

www.ingramcontent.com/pod-product-compliance
Lightning Source LLC
LaVergne TN
LVHW051040070526
838201LV00066B/4869